LOOK AND FIND®

Cover illustration by
John Kurtz Studios

Illustrated by Jamie Diaz Studios

©Disney Enterprises, Inc.

Published by
Louis Weber, C.E.O., Publications International, Ltd.
7373 North Cicero Avenue, Lincolnwood, Illinois 60712

Ground Floor, 59 Gloucester Place, London W1U 8JJ

www.pilbooks.com

Manufactured in China.

8 7 6 5 4 3 2 1

ISBN 0-7853-9763-9

publications international, ltd.

Cinderella

Dear Diary,

The most amazing thing happened today! Just when I thought that I would miss the Prince's ball, my Fairy Godmother appeared in the garden. She told me that she would help me get to the ball on time, but that I need to find these unusual things.

A carriage horse

A magic wand

Jaq

This mouse

This pumpkin

This mouse

Gus

Belle

Dear Diary,

I'm so homesick, how could I possibly eat? Lumiere and Mrs. Potts have gone to so much trouble, but I'm just not hungry. Among all the snacks and desserts, there are a couple unusual things I sure haven't seen before. Have you?

French bread

Angel food cake

Caesar salad

Chilled asparagus

Strawberry shortcake

Aged cheese

Chicken à la king

Snow White

Oh, Diary!

What a mess! The forest animals led me to a charming cottage tucked away in the woods. It belongs to seven very untidy Dwarfs! I better get to work and start cleaning. Look at all the Dwarfs' belongings that need to be put away.

Grumpy's rocks

Bashful's toy hedgehog

Sneezy's flowers

Sleepy's blanket

Doc's inkwell

Dopey's alarm clock

Happy's chest

Ariel

Dear Diary,

Eric and I were married today. It was a celebration like none ever seen on land or under the sea! It was a fairy-tale wedding, and I'm ready to embark on a fairy-tale honeymoon. Look at all the friends who came to wish Eric and me a happy ever-after!

King Triton

Carlotta

Scuttle

Grimsby

Flounder

Chef Louie

Sebastian

Max

Sleeping Beauty

Oh, Diary!

Today is my sixteenth birthday. I am so excited! Not only have I met the man of my dreams, but my forest friends have thrown me a birthday party. Just look and see all the wonderful gifts they have made!

Walking stick

Acorn earrings

Wall plaque

Bracelet

Upside-down cake

Birthday crown

Berry necklace

Jasmine

Dear Diary,

Most people are excited about birthdays, but not me. The law says that I have to marry a prince before my next birthday, but I don't want to. I'm not ready or interested in marrying anyone yet! And you should see some of the characters who have gathered in the palace garden. None of them are my type!

Prince
Ima Stinker

Prince
Abracadabra

Prince Havallama

Prince
Jim Nastic

Prince
Chocolotts

Prince
Nick Nack

Mulan

Dear Diary,

Today I meet the matchmaker. It's important that I bring honor and dignity to my family. This is such a very special day, but I'm a little late — as always! In all this confusion, I lost a few items. Look around this busy scene and help me gather these things every woman needs.

A pendant for balance

An apple for serenity

This fan

Beads of jade for beauty

My special comb

A cricket for luck

This parasol

Pocahontas

Dear Diary,

John Smith and I had a beautiful day walking and talking. I wanted to share with him the many valuable lessons I've learned from nature. I think he finally understands. How could he not? The swirling wind is quite a teacher! Look at all the things the wind carries to show us how everything is connected and that life is a circle that never ends.

Bear paw

Yellow bird

Butterfly

Shell

Eagle feather

Blue jay feather

Footprint

Wedding bells are ringing over land and sea for Ariel and Eric! Can you find these other "bells" at their wedding?

☐ Barbells
☐ A Southern belle
☐ Bell-bottoms
☐ A bell pepper
☐ A belly flop
☐ A blue bell

Go to where John Smith learns things he never knew. Find the animals that match these facts.

☐ It plays dead if it thinks it is in danger.
☐ It is a member of the same family as the dog.
☐ It sheds its skin as it grows.
☐ It hunts at night with strong, sharp talons.

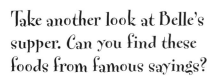
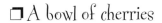

In the palace garden, Jasmine found that the suitors didn't suit her, but she loved their horses. Find these other horse things.

☐ Horse scents
☐ Horse thief
☐ Horse fly
☐ Trojan horse
☐ Horse hide
☐ Horse and buggy

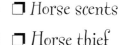

Take another look at Belle's supper. Can you find these foods from famous sayings?

☐ A bowl of cherries
☐ Spilled milk
☐ A flat pancake
☐ A cool cucumber
☐ A crumbling cookie
☐ A hat with a bite out of it
☐ A pickle
☐ Sour grapes

Can you spot these musicians who have come to serenade Sleeping Beauty?

❏ A bird quartet
❏ A squirrel with maracas
❏ A frog chorus
❏ A mushroom-playing skunk

Although most of the animals are assisting Snow White in tidying up the Dwarfs' cottage, a number of them aren't exactly helping. Can you find these animals that are taking a cleaning break?

❏ One juggling bunny
❏ Two teeter-tottering friends
❏ One tightrope walker
❏ Three jump-roping squirrels
❏ Two soap-sliding bunnies

Cinderella enjoys working in the garden because the animals are such good company and the flowers are so beautiful. Go back and stroll through the garden to find these flower arrangements.

❏ A basket of flowers
❏ A tiara of flowers
❏ Flower garland
❏ A bouquet of flowers

Mulan isn't the only one who has come to meet the matchmaker. Can you spot these people and animals who have gone to a lot of trouble to wait their turn?

❏ A well-groomed dog
❏ An elegant duck
❏ The fancy-fan man
❏ The powder-puff woman